FIELD HOLLERS

FIELD HOLLERS

Iván Argüelles & Solomon Rino

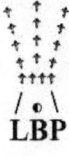
LBP

2021

Field Hollers

Iván Argüelles & Solomon Rino © 2021

San Francisco & Berkeley, California

Cover by C. Mehrl Bennett

ISBN: 9781938521768

https://www.lulu.com/spotlight/lunabisonteprods

Luna Bisonte Prods
137 Leland Ave
Columbus OH 43214 USA

for Maximilian Anton Argüelles

TWIN: *Right cheek pressed to window outdoors.* TWIN: *Left cheek pressed to same window indoors.* TWIN: *Outdoors left palm placed to window.* TWIN: *Indoors right palm placed to window. Neither can be heard by the other.*

TWIN: What if there were an exit with no labyrinth, depths where light is an excuse for sleep, and longing the nature of being? To proceed gather threads of the already shared or half-illumined, saga of hiding during the pest in a macaronic pas-tiche of idioms and dialects, phonology of the dispossessed and build on a metronome of bricks, measuring the kaleidoscope of musical exchange between prayer and stutter.

TWIN: Insomnia and aggravation, these are the clues to the poem's germination, followed by the ineffable block of marble addressing the leaf stuck to the darkened windowpane. Dawn too will come, in an epiphany as much as denial. Speech act best defined as the 13th form of clinical aphasia.

TWIN: What if there were infinite exits denied, a mowed field where the cameraman faints and films the sky, wakes in a house that he built but cannot enter nor leave as all doors creak open and close? Lens of turgid majesty without touch like memory groping toward an indifferent swan. Stutter lakes never rivers.

TWIN: Thisness of a stone ocean-weary silently truth telling like a planet on stilts. Cairns the only verity in toppling. Speech always a falling away. The great orator marble mouthed speaking against speech to avoid the impediment the only instance of language that is holy.

Twins change position without moving.

TWIN: Communication is only a barrier, hands in an imagined atmosphere of dialogue and repercussion. Echoes that resist being cataloged as pronominal directions. If you add to the plural of water and devise an atrocious engine I can ponder as to what illusory decibel mind belongs, shadowy entrails of identity and miscomprehension, sudden act of creation, budding nonsense of interstices and approximation to the prefixes to sound. No meaning but in the punctuations of silence. If this makes sense, I am moving in the wrong dimension.

TWIN: Cavernous air, repository of all sounds possible and impossible, I shake in this demonic suction of vowel and shoreline, this foreseeable demonstration of utter loss. Did you see the comet by day tailing its own lesson of gravity, rising like Lazarus from his tomb of consonants? Breath is conjecture, lamentation is the only depth. Everything else is an afternoon in the anitpodes. Be with me!

One twin turns upside down, as if a playing card. Removes ear, placing it on an udder. In the other ear hears a thumb brush gently.

TWIN: Hands held in every gift never opened, palms seek justice in epistrophes butter-churned flesh-odor pushing with one hand rosary in the other, yellow and onyx a birthmark in a barrel. Sing into wood the only constant a lamp at the base of repercussion. Intestines belong to the drum and the swooning vulture resounds full of brains and barley flour. Mind in flight take this skull from me virtuous shitter of stupas.

TWIN: Stalagmites recede emigrating from throated resound to a dandelion grandmother-haired winded. A larynx without deposit like the erosion of hoodoos becoming men. Fingerprints on the throat of the mumbler disavow secrets. A lattice is never a child however overgrown, but speaks in chattering net the sob. Your cheek pales in nowhere to go as does mine. Up and down in stasis the only hymnal.

TWIN: Umbrellas pile ever open guarding from the tower reaches of cobbled lallation. Say I to every lapel flower toppling undipped in death pangs a promise. Wanted to rub the rain, the terror in occasions, anarchy of the gaping mouth in silence. Wanted to return silk to the worm, unweaving this jacket at the altar shivering. Wanted to wet the bell ocean its only clapper. What is more than a helmet full of water?

TWIN: Convexities of atmosphere, blotted black homophone of the sun, acrostics of cloud and distance, wherever you look there is an apogee like the chaconne of the endless bow. Nothing is foreseeable only the distinctions of phoneme in their regrettable sequence we call human endeavor. Speech act of marble, diphthongs worn like head-gear among the ancients. Cothurn and unfolding stocking, mouth full of redundancies and clematis vine. Abide with me.

TWIN: Democratic fictions of air, divisible half and then subtracted from noon, when statues learn to grieve and the civil war cannon of the Court House fires off its salvo and litanies. If you put your ear to stone you can hear the origins, the soils of distance and memory. Ink blotter and bleak fiction of letters, erasures and the depilatory of thought, all in conjunction with a new moon, a novel moaning in the rushes. Light me up no more.

TWIN: *dies wandering in indefinite sleep churning colloidal seas with a ladle of melting lead and whooping hollers.*

TWIN: I am a camera, the divided between the sexes of the sky cloud. For me summer is a lens, azure tinted and full of haze, like the day building came down and we could not find hands enough to lift the brow. Incandescence in the one virtue, the others are smoke smothered in a hill of mute consonants. Philology is no guide. My throat is blue from budding underground. Let none with me aide.

TWIN: I am the master-negative, in which all reflux is the opposite of blank, white repercussion in an echo of ears. The canyon below the bottom step, don't go there. The asphalt ribbon is the sound to follow far into the dissonance of a future two days dead already. Alphanumeric regrets, *pentimento* and sovereign grief. Mutilated shadows crawling sideways up the destroyed tenement of Shiva. Lock me in your harm.

TWIN: Envy the threshing floor each grain above us as idioms never unite. Arrow pierced cheeks stumble about the tongue posing questions: *Which cloth robes you? How long undead? Are you certain?* Sieves stretched with calfskin serenade rake and plow. Sky headstands blue kernels in kettles until all consume light and are silent.

TWIN: Music leavens dough under the piano this is culture swimming upward well baked in Phlegethon cascades. To release is to capture a *legato* of the latent image stained with exquisite jam. Torches forgive caves their lack of thrones, as rewind moves forward until poof a picnic in utter black photographed by a monarch. The only print is in windowed bitumen.

TWIN: Dreadlocks pile on the floor cliffward continue to pile eclipsing *thangkas*: crag-clatter in the microcosm of every lock learning to speak. Giving song to the upside-down climber seeking pubic hair of gods to nest in. There dance is constant as is sleep. Only the palimpsest is read and *stretto* never returns. Is this unparsable reverence?

TWIN: Cairns are a form of speech, stones ululate at the midnight hour. Cliffs are the ultimate punctuation, horses and adders and elephants of pure light trying to pass through the ocean's archaic eye. Vowels or rock formation, how dare we cross with trousers rolled up, a hundred years after the Waste Land. That is not a question but a fugue, the darkness it takes to howl, and frigates of electricity on the bare arm. Do we really understand a painting unless it hangs on the penultimate wall of the Museum? It scratches my head to think, and splotches of acrylic and vodka hidden in the stitching of the Dutch doll thrown into the Gowanus canal last Sunday. Frozen. Push me into the ignition.

Wheedling and whistling into the empty arm-brace secrets of the other brace rebirths TWIN.

TWIN: Hit cymbals with baskets of snakes, the trap kit split overflows adders, the snare Cleopatra's sigh. Unhoused we writhe. To dream of a street hole cover receding as you plummet at immeasurable speed and wake to indigenous voices. Time without envy riffing in impossible ceremony drinking milk from a gong without mallet. No seasons, never seasons.

TWIN: Just back from the death-after-death, so many houses each more house than the other and the windows all indolent with dying. Seasons on the margin of a single phoneme that is supposed to represent space before time. Can't help having this nauseous feeling that we've been in this shipwreck before. Cliffs and ululations, somber interstices, the ocean barking like a hyena at the umbratile moon. So long since we had the hiccoughs and the movie hasn't even started. Dye my hair fuchsia.

TWIN: *Merry and dronke wee both*, little lads a pissing up stream, night rumors. Aghast the drawings we stare, the stars the bleary countenances we peer. Did ever liffle blossom bloom its bosom to sleep, nor did divine rivers their beds still the deep. Heaps of ire and envy, the shadows have their walls, and the walls their entity of longing. My stutter's gone chrome and flickers glyphs apart from sacred bone. Least is a tittle shall we part and grieve. The throne's gone empty.

TWIN: *And holofernes was mery & dranke so moche wyn that he never dranke so moche in one day in all hys lyf, & was dronken. And at even whan it was nyght olofernes wente vnto hys bedde, and vago brought Judith in to his chambre and closid the dore. And whan Judith was allone in the chambre* she quilted a shroud a narrowing kern into which she bathed and drying herself the impression of her flesh was misspelled. Heads putted into skittle alleys of witness a pharmakon. Circles once tattooed scream meter-flayed into conches and drink from them.

TWIN *and* TWIN *speak simultaneously a ruckus of bleating harps.*

TWIN *and* TWIN: Anaphora each jealous of the next: Don't send the letter, I haven't written it yet: Parables seek light endlessly, what is to be learned?: The ecumene vast as it is, Han's portals to the shaking pillars of Palmyra. Inhabit we then it: Parataxis towers, top middle bottom, unaware of architecture: Lissome parts a diddled fane, the priest lie dronken miseries, daisies in the crupper of their hands, a mantle bleeding: Hearthward the goat's heart aorta broken with a twist for the gods in the palm of stammer: Stagecraft lean leftward here, branching syntax into sleep's back pocket. If you take it out to read, it's only a lantern burnt: Read knuckled secrets in syntagms down for the count like boxing centipedes: It's what was on the refrigerator door, a refinery of archaic half-words, lexicon and haberdashery of Hecate: Leave one home dark then we can decipher the scream: Head is heavy with the sun's black homophones, rising risen ridden.

TWIN(S) *again speak retrograde.*

TWIN: A kettle, a kennel of fish, twyformed bracken weir we must step. And careful not to cradle the wrong apostrophe, the dwindling rumor of asterisks. If only we could perpetuate the stone of summer, the golf course where the dead bury their fingers. It is up to us, profligates weary and wary of the way home to return, ultimately and without sound-bites, the atrocious navigation of mind through epics of sand, the symbol of blindness. Don't forget to number me, Mummer.

TWIN: Herdsman of the Ur ox dies an aurochs in a forest overgrown in expansive grief his last words: "I lost all that I…" Drone of the hive splits the skull into two rafts carrying honey to the bride who asks, "Will you can you undo me?" DRONE: Ontogeny envies velvet you (*Stage front center*) uncurtained in (*To stage front right*) antimony (*To stage front left*) spit paper dunes (*curtain*).

TWIN: Each twinkling star Lamia's groan in night sky we are all bastards drowned. Silverfish groins lineage of the pen. We cannot kill love so inky riverbanks scatter lament in papyrus fragments: what remains? Goodbye child of green winter, is anything possible? Will you, can you be written to return?

TWIN: Me is the ancient vowel. You is the thrum-thrum drone of monotonous death. Call and response from meadow to ravished Warsaw ghetto. Mine was the first bride, all grinning tooth and skull, a pear tree for a surname and rites of Jobs' Daughters spreading down to anklets in dripping splendor. Yours was the second bride, starbright from the loins of the Lithuanian Luftwaffe. Next of kin, hairdressers in black lipstick. Fellatio and street games in the heat attack of the Spider-women, bad Spanish pronunciation and drowning in gastric reflux.
Fuck all poetry!

TWIN: Back from the other world, nether vowels, twysome bits of sound a big screen version of Omega, all that gloss on her lips, too. Grief is the plunge she splits into hives, three hemi-spheres at a time. Nothing rhymes, space is an abstract noun with nothing to fill its void. Blind to have every moment I ever lost sorrowing back, unless it's you, my young dividend. Odd the way an echo has a way of turning into metal all sheen in the simmering glow of its own homophone, black and irreverent.
Know thyself.

TWIN: Effect without cause Styx foghorns: Jump ship! Jump ship! The damned cannot swim, none of us can, hugging planks we endear sucking sap from knots as if breasts. The dead do not pray forever in prayer singing: *Since I've Laid My Burden Down*. No moon no tide only the phlegmatic call: "Where have you led me now?" Kick and kick and kick cascades never apologize. Mother on the bank above morganatic how many dawns will you scream into your gift?

TWIN: Reclaim foreskins and like angels wear them as rings, as nuns wear the foreskin of Christ. Wedded to end eschatology inscribe your ring with: "Stain mired in ewe-lipped hours, the rhubarb-dove molts." Nona punches the red radio in which Nonno drowned bringing him back to bootlegging. Rustling through his chest I found bocce balls as hearts, uncles playing grabass with your throw, trousers belted to
the nipples, where is your penis?

TWIN: Adverse as a water with nowhere to shore. Given the tombstone around our necks, I'd say its time to Plunge. Derricks cannot lift us, nor a prayer. It is with isosceles triangles that the priest circumcises the air winnowing over our heads. A raft and a plucked lyre, downstream to Hades, and isn't she the One! Plump and hair a bit over-fried, auburn turning to deep rust. She could have been the bride of each or the other of us, two at a time. Turn the hot water off.

TWIN: No holler today the page winded turning on rooftops of underground hollows where the insurgent word sweats out, out the alien. Stint the heart underpainted ochre overpainted cobalt, impasto then, then collage of cuttings, how to spread cages? Towers middle out to plastic Babel, can I but labor in trampled palms, when, when can I go back to frescoes of outlawed Tuesdays? Free is the only dirty word, the holy word is standpipe. Standpipe the stranger until he paints your portrait paintbrush between his teeth.

TWIN: Spot paper fumes floating in the meditative airs, windsquirms, splashes of dead atmosphere the size of India's rump. Can't you leave it alone, always fidgeting, rustling through those old documents, space-cadet stuff, Mayan warriors who didn't turn their taxes in. Shit, you know. Don't open the bottom drawer, full of old tape-cassettes, garage music from the early '80's, horse-manure set to a band of fiddle strings. Girls who use a perfume called opium, heady stuff. It's enough to know we're at a cultural dead-end, no space to alleviate the rhyme tags of a marginal discourse on the death of Sokrates. Amen.

TWIN: Center leaves windward stalking speech acts in a muddle, half priced to right. Awkward boats lesions and stammers wave and weave then plundered the assize, taxes thumbs down. If we cold but addle the small and slightly battered huff, a hat a jam an instrument of play the bold. And remember the morgue's first day, the play of light the slanted sun nowhere a plight, each blackened seed an eternity to live. I cry to call a shift's red depth in tone, and Greek the swarm of bees they were, and lonesome the last to buzz and hum. Seek the stoned pit, no letter ever gets home.

TWIN *and* TWIN *overlap tonguey rapping.*

TWIN *and* TWIN: Fathered by whom mother's brother cannot does not escape, offers no kiss only a glass that does not hold the whole bottle of wine spilling staining the tablecloth with lipstick: Palming off sealskins, oil traders, future adventurers on the Silk Road, hawking bad wares, batik and tie-die shirts manufactured in Jakarta sweat shops, stooping to light a match to see what comes off: The snake is scissored, its blood pressed into a glass of white whisky headless wriggles consonant with the earthquake I drink: Then they talk of *houris* and *apsarases* and the colloidal nymphs of when they shared the same womb. Disasters of a necessity come in twos: Quiver less. Hands extended take me in your arms to kill me twice *in girum* I am defenseless: Advent of pseudo-Christs, white-rose petroleum jelly, and the Ring Saga, played on the radio between 4 and 4:15 PM daily: Carmen never died, nor did Desdemona she breathes again the theater Relâche: Paunch hits Juicy and Citizen baby rattles the coop with hints Poetry from the Lake Country. All arpeggios suffer: Re-wind the Victrola again, Please.

TWIN(S) *again speak retrograde.*

TWIN: TRANCE says Daddy his body swells and shirt bursts to a cuckoo-clock chiming simultaneously little couples on tracks singing *Ave...* trance removes complete demolition surround surrounds the curse lapping fire all applaud blowing mouthfuls of liquor into pots boiling rapeseed and collapse the explosion with their drums hymens still. trance in red purification knife to the flame to the tongue kisses the water deity. trance collapses out of trance with the turn of each page entranced only by the text read. Heartbeats come quadruped if we burn silk and flour.

TWIN: Brothered by a father placated by a desire to amorphous genetic destiny, and failed on so many levels to find the right key, magnum qua nothing of stretch and die. The subject has no predicate and the silverfish are whining through drivel after drivel of pre-paginated texts about heat cycles. Almost mustered by a mother who didn't quite fix her scrabble board in time, only to find cul-de-sacs galore in the fabled north country where the Ojibway get fixing to meet the Big Manitou in the sky. Pearls of beer frown the forehead, teenage episodes re-lived on acid and peyote. Gives you the screaming jimmies, crawl up and down the falsetto frosted wallpaper. Hemispheres come in threes. It's the insect in every-man that brings out the drama on his foreskin. Get ready to blow, Madonna's back in town all widgeted up in copies of her own skin, humming the prelude to Lohengrin in her fish-net stocking underwear. Don't write home!

TWIN: *Right-side matricide*, TWIN: *Left-side matricide*.
MOTHER *between* Lachrymose *as in* Pergolesi's *Stabat Mater*.

TWIN: What's an epitaph but a flower that has forgotten how to read. An inkling if not the underworld where Persephone darns her socks and dries her hair in the Stygian dank. Why was it me who had to geminate, flowering two precise buds, identities stolen from an injunction, a pool of theories about the baseness of the soul entering the body. Let the emperor Hadrian ponder that little vague thing, wingless flitting in fear of the great DDT spray of the heavens.

TWIN: All glass cries for haecceity tinted in Empoli green or patinas of tremor this window waltzes repaired again guillotined again widow resists outline as see-through shoots through our mutter engraved only with typos *i iu iu oe e ouiu ii* why the end remembers holding paling hands maypole ribbons or penny whistlers wreathed in 3-d glasses.

TWIN *telephones* TWIN: Let's trade faces (*trade faces still Identical*) exchange right hands for left (*exchange hands same chiromancy*) loosen foot from ankle, (*feet fall toes remain*) load the shoulder with that express pound of grief (*shoulders never slough*): Looking down from the cloud in the rain one never sees faces only stupas pacing without relics: It's ages since the phone was developed with its idiocy of vowels in rotation, Platonic sub-terfuge meant to disguise the wheels of thought: "*Que el vent morat apaga amb la seva ombra*" ideas should be compared to the square root of one, mystical counterfeit of ontological weight, gravity in reverse, sleep as if space didn't exist: I caress my cheek caressing yours (*thumbs to cheeks*) sleep doubled always fitful as one must keep watch when in love: Troubled by the mire and maze of memory, what was the name of that river made of cigarettes?: The river of swords where we skipped cobblestones that never stopped aimed at the *Ancien Régime*: Each time we started walking home, like the time we stole the 3 Musketeer candy bars from the drug store, and got caught. It's a good thing mom and dad were in their siesta down in Teotihuacan, ca. 100 CE: Are we in their nap now?

TWIN: I have forgotten your telephone number no mnemonic since Simonides in this "whorish othertime" yet squat to squat see *dioscuri* my reflection topples home. Tiles fly when named in the basement with Mother watching the tornado on television about to take the house down, she screams, "Why do you speak?" (*Roof falls floor tiles go up window remains*). We cannot answer on our knees hunched over hands to napes as we were trained yet glance, and chuckle.

TWIN: This *gior-nata* that never dries has no outline never another day never a way out. At San Marco I turn lynched in velvet ropes every cell a cinema let the assistants paint. Actors masked arc always exiled body loses body deprived of image I tie your blindfold. Gagged *angelico* make some noise like a jack in the box or "reciprocal inference of series." Stand apart from you becoming you incarnations do not jive step away from the earth earth-bound man in the light of the projector wander.

TWINS *untwin. Retwin. Repeat.*

TWIN: The wind is putting out all of us, no time for a nap, nor for the cumbersome stupas of ash and cinders we have to carry to the goal posts where it's always Friday night game-time. Tom-toms and Indian love shouts, cries from the left shoulder to the right, half hidden truant eyes, which is yours which is thine. Medical notions of air, glucose and styrofoam adjectives, verbal twitches in the right knee, trying desperately to express its covert reaction to birth. A hide, two melons, the deer that drowned in Diana's cucumber-colored pool, and the lasses all agasp. Can it be one twin forgot the other's name?

TWIN: Let's try this, trade masks again but turn them inside out and see who resembles the other the most. But don't use mirrors or quartz or any other kind of mercurial device. Shattered illusions always follow the letter *kappa*, odd, isn't it? I promised years ago to take mother to Brazil, but she always thought you were more spiritually pure. Probably because you took less time to deliver newspapers than I did. Unfortunately, she got dementia and didn't recognize it was you who was denigrating the dates on the calendar. It was all happening in the North Woods, dynamic frescos of white on white, blizzards frosts and snowfalls of epic proportions. When she died she asked for one more cigarette, the kind Saint Teresa smoked when she posed for Bernini.

TWIN: The automaton never laughs when holding handfuls of soil he knows how he's rigged but what of this? Uncut, unhewn, sees it fall in swerve and swoons. In this negative witnessing no childhood memories receiving and interpreting impressions as within a vessel. Change the channel Worm to the puppet-show without strings, heaps on heaps ever boxed like fishing tackle. Medusa fell in love when she wore hats with women braiding their hair. She made cairns of them. What guide earth, what guide?

TWIN: If only we could worm and wriggle out of these shadows, they keep cropping up on walls when least expected. A universe apart between snowflakes and the vowel each one is supposed, required to represent, and it all hits the concrete and melts. Like the time they dragged us up from the Floating Gardens to the terraces behind the hospital where we were born, and winter spread its cascade of obliterable consonants all pronounced with the tip of the tongue outside the mouth. From there to the Trick Shoppe across the street from the hospital was no ordinary leap, but one not of faith but of sheer denial. Heat wound its band around our temples, and the tighter it got the louder the air sounded, cavernous and Olympian with pygmies banging their clackers at the birth of Zeus. Funny little apostrophes totally outside the legend of Grammar.

TWIN: Speaking of puppets what are you doing with that dead baby? String after string of interrupted speech acts, marmoreal and desiccated. If talk could walk, how many vowels would it need? You're full of inanities today, music all puffy and grown up sounding, like it needs a Burma after-shave ad. It comes down to childhood every time, and only that, a blade of grass, a broken tooth, someone's idea of a kite two-faced and stringless dangling in a proportion of air that has no stage-direction. And always the funny little non-sequiturs, fishing on a deserted lake with Grand-pa, flush and carmine with an overdose of dandelion wine. Stick your foot in the bag and press down really hard before you get to China. With the right know-how you can actually put all of New York City in a thimbleful of water. Really.

TWIN: Cassandra and Tiresias cut the gigue knit and purl correct me. Danced to Lord Invader in bay "throw out that damn baby." Are origins necessary? Cassandra's daughter was met with verity but had no tongue Tiresias' son could see the tv call me little one. Do you swaddle in quilt to outlie violence or is violence in the stitch? This three-legged race yarned in testimony without a clue. Chase the ellipses.

TWIN: Cassandra's harp, Cadmus' stolen letters, birds' feet quills pinnacles and invisible ink, death ultimately like the time we divided by three and no one won on that lonely hill where the playground swings rusted before our eyes. Later it got darker before it should have, we reckoned the one mourning dove we heard was telling us to go back to California. Snow to the contrary we watched the first tulips eke their effervescent bright-hued heads out from the cold into the purloined light of still another false April. Soon copies of ourselves using prefixes to Sanskrit verbs for mouths came to tug on our shadows. Get along Little Doggie!

(*Curtain*).

TWIN: The tooth sower nightly embraces his sow zips himself into a burlap bag (the bag called Arepo) doesn't want anyone to know he lacks an arm and a scythe shuffles to the opera where he twists and turns in the loge waiting for that light, that light to teethe on. The orchestra is simply an army of 32 holding 64 tortoise shells aflame and the soloists are never alone. The baton unmanned chews and spits in Phoenician tripods is this a beginning? Which divines what holds never any balustrades never?

TWIN: Thrust into my.

Field Hollers was born of insomnia, trading stanzas largely predawn, back and forth before light harrowed.

Iván Argüelles and Solomon Rino, 2021